Blessed Art Thou Among Women

Reflections on Mary in Our World Today

EDITORS

Cynthia Fox

Joshua Simon

Robert Sullivan

ART EDITORS

Melanie deForest

Vivette Porges

MACMILLAN • USA

To my beautiful godfather, Skipper Dunn—C.F.

+

To my mother—M.D.

+

To my parents, Lucie and P.P.P., and in memory of our Mary—V.P.

+

To my wife, Miriam—J.S.

+

To two Lucilles, a Mary and a Marie, loving mothers all—R.S.

MACMILLAN
A Simon & Schuster Macmillan Company
1633 Broadway
New York, NY 10019

Library of Congress Cataloging-in-Publication Data
Who do you say that I am? : reflections on Jesus in our world today /
[compiled by] Vivette Porges, Joshua Simon, Robert Sullivan.
p. cm.
ISBN 0-02-861995-1
1. Jesus Christ—Person and offices—Quotations, maxims, etc.
I. Sullivan, Robert
BT205.W47 1996   96-23048
232—dc20   CIP

Book design by Nick Anderson

Manufactured in the United States of America

10 9 8 7 6 5 4 3 2 1

✠ ACKNOWLEDGMENTS

The authors would like to thank their colleagues at *LIFE* magazine, especially former managing editor Dan Okrent, who allowed them to plumb the mystery of Mary in *LIFE*'s pages; current managing editor Jay Lovinger, who deftly shaped *LIFE*'s cover story on the mystery of Mary; and art director Tom Bentkowski along with photographer Len Jenshel, whose visual evocation of the mystery of Mary graced that magazine and graces this book. They would also like to acknowledge the faith, talent and guidance of their editors at Macmillan: John Michel, who brought the volumes on Jesus and Mary to the imprint; and Olga Moya and Natalie Chapman, who shepherded this latest effort to completion. Thanks go as well to the authors' agent at International Creative Management, Sloan Harris, who went the extra mile to assure that this meditation on Mary saw the light of day.

And, of course, our deepest gratitude goes to all the fine thinkers who took the time to share their thoughts on Mary with us. With us... and now with our readers.

Saint Mary della Misericordia, Piero della Francesca

✪ introduction

"Blessed art thou among women"

Luke 1:28

That many of us feel a need for Mary, the Blessed Mother, the Mother of Jesus, is indisputable. Why we need Mary, and what we hope to receive from Mary—these are more involved considerations. "We live in a society where iron and cement triumph," says Father Stefano De Fiores, professor of Historical Mariology at the Pontifical Gregorian University in Rome. "Mary is an irreproachable figure esthetically, and responds to two great needs in such a society. For belonging. And for tenderness."

Can it possibly be as simple as that? For some, it can be. Mary soothes, and that is enough. For others, the issue of Mary—the concept of Mary, the person who was Mary, the presence of Mary today—is infinitely more complex.

The authors of the book you hold in your hands learned this for a certainty when we started investigating and interviewing for this volume. First, we became acutely aware of how scant the contemporaneous, documentary evidence is regarding Mary. When we assembled our earlier book, *Who Do You Say That I Am?: Reflections on Jesus in Our World Today*, we had, at least, the wealth of history and anecdote contained in the Synoptic Gospels, the Gospel of John, and related apocrypha. Mary's appearances in those texts are few indeed, and much of what we now know—or think we know—about Christ's mother was not written until long after her life on Earth.

Because of this, we have decided to take a slightly different tack with *Blessed Art Thou Among Women* from the one we followed in *Who Do You Say That I Am?* Instead of relying exclusively on Biblical quotations from the marvelously poetic King James Bible to establish a narrative—and to lend context to the testimony of our many interview subjects—we will present, in each section of this book, a brief critical discussion of the aspect of Mary that we are to consider. This will afford the reader some history, some perspective, and—again—some context.

We do this because there is so very little Bible-era journalism regarding Mary, and also because it is an exercise that we have recently been engaged in. For the December 1996 cover story in *LIFE* magazine, the authors investigated the mystery of Mary and produced a prize-winning feature. We learned much in working on that story, and would like to share the fruits of our efforts with the readers of this book. Therefore, with some modifications, passages from the *LIFE* piece will serve to introduce the several faces of Mary in our world, and to discuss the significance they have had, yesterday, today, and tomorrow.

You will notice, in some of these excerpts, the first-person-singular pronoun. It is, we would argue, in keeping with the spirit of this book. The *LIFE* piece, which was assembled by the five of us, was written by Robert Sullivan. The magazine's meditation on Mary became, ultimately, personal as well as journalistic, subjective as well as objective.

This is what our modest volumes are all about: the personal reflection, the subjective view. What does Jesus mean to each of us? What does Mary mean—to the American and the African; the Catholic, the Protestant, the Buddhist, the Hindu and the Jew; the clergy and the laity; the scholar and the novitiate; the deep-believer and the casual believer?

Moreover, how do the interpretations of others differ from, inform, support or advance a reader's own opinion? What we hope to encourage, in the current case, is a single, simple meditation.

What does Mary mean to me?

The Mystery of Mary

The young Jewish girl goes to the stone synagogue in Nazareth. She offers devotions in the small women's section adjacent to the main prayer hall. In chorus with other congregants, the girl recites psalms and absorbs their lessons: "Abandon yourself to God." One extraordinary day she is visited by an angel who asks if she'll play a part in the birth of God's son. She answers yes. Two thousand years ago she makes her way with her husband, Joseph, a carpenter, to a village called Bethlehem. In a stable (for the inn is filled) they celebrate the birth of a son. They lay the infant in a feeding stall, and name him Yeshua—in Greek, Jesus. She raises Jesus to be a strong, brave young man, a leader of other men. This is the story of Miriam— or Mary—of Nazareth. This is all we really know.

"You could copy on an eight-and-a-half-by-eleven sheet everything there is about Mary in the New Testament," says Jaroslav Pelikan, president of The American Academy of Arts and Sciences and author of *Mary Through the Centuries*. "Now, with Jesus, you can know more about any player in the NBA than about Jesus. But at least with Jesus there's the material in the four Gospels. With Mary—well, to get from such skimpy evidence to what she has become is an astonishing example of how an idea can develop out of small beginnings."

The "idea" of Mary, so sparely drawn and therefore so open to interpretation, has roller-coastered through 2,000 years of Christian history, alternately elevated and demoted by the Catholic hierarchy, shunned and praised by the Protestant. But if her official standing has been in constant flux, her public image has been on a two-millennium-long rise. Mary belongs not to the priests but to the

Annunciation, Sandro Botticelli

people. No matter what has been decreed in a given era, the popular passion for her has remained resolute. Her disciples—her congregation, her soldiers—have adamantly refused to let Mary recede.

Why? What do they so vitally require from this most famous of mother figures? How has she, once an unknown, grown to be such an immense personality? Why are two billion Hail Marys said daily? Why did five million people, many non-Christian, visit Lourdes this year to drink the healing waters? Why did more than ten million trek to Guadalupe to pray to Our Lady? Why is it thought that more girls have been named for Mary than for any other historical figure? Why the apparitions? Why the need to talk with her? Why are Mary hymns creeping into Methodist songbooks? How can it be that Mary adorns the banners of liberals who seek a greater role for women in all churches, and also those of conservatives who would keep ministries all-male?

What is it about Mary?

Hail Mary, full of grace, the Lord is with thee.

Blessed art thou among women And blessed is the fruit of thy womb, Jesus...

In thinking back on my Roman Catholic upbringing, as a meditation upon the mystery of Mary inevitably forces me to do, I realize that both ideas—Mary and Catholicism—were put before me simultaneously with this prayer. I assumed my mother gave me this prayer first, even before the Lord's Prayer, because it was shortest. Or, perhaps, so I could get some use out of my plastic rosary.

Maybe these were the reasons. But now I wonder if Mary's prayer came early to guide me gently to the faith, to allow me an unforbidding avenue to heaven—to God. In the twelfth century the great theologian Bernard of Clairvaux wrote, "If you fear the Father, go to the Son, if you fear the Son, go to the Mother." I learned to go to the Mother, and I went—willingly, confidently, happily.

Robert Sullivan, LIFE *magazine, December 1996*

The Annunciation, Leonardo da Vinci

The Annunciation, Henry Ossawa Tanner

And the angel came in unto her, and said, Hail, thou art highly favoured, the Lord is with thee: blessed art thou among women.

And when she saw him, she was troubled at his saying, and cast in her mind what manner of salutation this should be.

And the angel said unto her, Fear not, Mary: for thou hast found favour with God.

And, behold, thou shalt conceive in thy womb, and bring forth a son, and shalt call his name Jesus.

He shall be great, and shall be called the Son of the Highest: and the Lord God shall give unto him the throne of his father David:

And he shall reign over the house of Jacob for ever; and of his kingdom there shall be no end.

Then said Mary unto the angel, How shall this be, seeing I know not a man?

And the angel answered and said unto her, The Holy Ghost shall come upon thee, and the power of the Highest shall overshadow thee: therefore also that holy thing which shall be born of thee shall be called the Son of God.

And, behold, thy cousin Elisabeth, she hath also conceived a son in her old age: and this is the sixth month with her, who was called barren.

For with God nothing shall be impossible.

And Mary said, Behold the handmaid of the Lord; be it unto me according to thy word. And the angel departed from her.

Luke 1:28-38

In a religion where the image is predominantly masculine, Mary has served as the female presence, a kind of a goddess figure, and the hinge between humanity and divinity.

Long before Mary, in the Neolithic period, there was the Great Mother—they've just discovered that one of the earliest icons of the divine was a naked female. This was an age when agriculture was being invented and fertility was a sacred force. The female at this point was the earliest image of the divine. There were scarcely any male images. It was only later, when manipulation and control became important, that masculine images of the divine became popular. Then there were male Gods as well. They began defeating the female Gods in quite hideous battles. Still, the Great Mother persisted and, in some senses perhaps, became Mary.

Karen Armstrong, *for seven years a Roman Catholic nun, now professor of Religion at Leo Baeck College in London, and author of* A History of God

Annunciation, Ann Rayme

There's no reference to Mary, the mother of Jesus, in any of the Pauline corpus that was written between 50 and 62 A.D. There's no positive reference to Mary the mother of Jesus in Mark, the First Gospel, written between 65 and 72. There are only two references to her in Mark, and both of them are negative. One, in chapter three, portrays her as thinking that Jesus is out of his mind and so she's going to take him away. You don't get a positive image of Mary until you get to the writings of Matthew, and that was done in the ninth decade. There's no Virgin introduced anywhere until the ninth decade. What happened historically is that by the turn of the first century Christianity was beginning to be interpreted within Mediterranean concepts. It was a neo-Platonic world—flesh was evil and spirit was good. Anything that connected Jesus with flesh was considered evil. He was spiritualized. And so Mary, his mother, is groomed to be an ideal, almost fleshless woman. She is declared Virgin.

John Spong, *Episcopal bishop of Newark, New Jersey,*
and author of Born of a Woman

I think the real trinity is father, mother, child. And that's the real trinitarian source of the universe, as discovered by all of the greatest mystics.

Andrew Harvey, *author of* The Return of the Mother *and* Mary's Vineyard

There just seems to be something about Mary that brings out the devotional in people. Even the great theologians, when it came to talking about Mary, ultimately it was as though they were talking about their mother.

Maurice Hamington, *professor and Women's Studies coordinator, Mount*
St. Mary's College, Los Angeles, California; and author of Hail Mary?

There is a wonderful intensity of devotion, an overpowering richness of language that you encounter when you study Mary's impact in the world. As an intellectual historian, I focus on concepts, theories, and doctrines. Studying the story of Mary obliged me to be aware that those concepts and theories do not begin to explore the fullness of what she has meant and continues to mean to so many people. Pascal said that "the heart has its reason that the mind knows not of," and Mary embodies that sentiment exactly.

Jaroslav Pelikan, *Sterling Professor of History Emeritus at Yale University*
in New Haven, Connecticut; president of the American Academy of Arts and
Sciences, and author of Mary Through the Centuries

She is a shadow in the Gospels. The evangelists enlist her to carry the burdens of their theology. Luke plants words of prophecy in her mouth. Matthew packs her off to the imagined safety of Egypt. John, who never calls her by name, portrays a meddlesome mother at Cana. Mark sends her into the streets to claim her son from madness and from public shame.

Who was this young woman? A dark-eyed Palestinian virgin, her black hair covered, her face burned brown by the sun. Unless her family owned a slave or two, she bore the burdens and small joys of the women of her time and place: fetching morning's water with the women at the well, baking bread, caring for her mother, sweeping away the dust of summer, sensing the moment when the breeze shifts and evening approaches. She searched among the stars, wondering.

This is how I picture Mary: short, squat, turbaned and tired, shaking her head and trying to hide a smile as her first-born—the diffident dreamer—wanders in late again for His chores. She points to the water jugs and sends Him off; the afternoon shift at the well is His.

It must have been very difficult for an ordinary woman to raise such a gifted, distracted child.

John R. Lanci, *Professor of Religious Studies, Stonehill College, North Easton, Massachusetts*

I believe God knew before the foundations of the world that He would choose her—just as He chooses us—not because she was any different from any other girl of that day, but because He knew her heart and faith.

She was a busy, dedicated, caring mother—but a mother. We see this evidenced at the wedding in Cana. When they needed more wine, she simply told Jesus to do something about it. Like any mother, she ignored his excuse and assumed he'd obey. I love what she and Joseph said to Jesus when he'd been lost for three days: "Why did you do this to us?" Just like parents today.

Patricia Pfeiffer, *author of the novel*
Above All Women: The Story of the Virgin Mary

The Arrival at Bethlehem, Luc-Oliver Merson

Under the ordinary methods of Biblical scholarship, but with a feminist perspective, I read the primary New Testament texts about her—the Infancy Narratives—in the following way. The first chapter of the Gospel of Matthew depicts Mary as a woman endangered by the attitudes, behaviors, and rules of the patriarchal society of her time. But she is defended in an angelic revelation to her husband Joseph, which calls her pregnancy "of the Holy Spirit." This phrase does not refer in antiquity to a miraculous conception. Joseph is urged to complete the marriage to her, and he does, accepting the child. Matthew comments that this fulfills the prediction that one who was a virgin will conceive the child called Immanuel, God-with-us. In the first chapter of the Gospel of Luke, Mary herself is the recipient of an angelic visitation in which she is told she will have a son who will be called "the Son of God," a phrase which also did not connote a miraculous conception. Instead of a response to her question about how this will come about, she is given reassurance of protection and empowerment by the Holy Spirit. The song put into her mouth, the Magnificat, voices the joy of a humiliated and vindicated woman as a sign of God's ultimate justice.

Between these accounts and the historical events is the stage of oral tradition—perhaps rooted in the memory of women and some courageous men—which did not blame Mary for the pregnancy and did not dismiss Jesus because of His heritage of illegitimacy. In the post–New Testament history of Christianity, this tradition was all but erased by the doctrine of a virginal conception, the doctrine, that is, of a nonsexual conception in which divine paternity replaced human paternity. Mary became seen as the Virgin Mother, a feminine ideal that is goddess-like but most often has not served to empower women.

Jane Schaberg, *Professor of Religious Studies and Women's Studies,*
University of Detroit Mercy

Early church sources, like Papias and Hegesippus, make it clear that Mary had *four children*, if not five: James, Simon, Judas, and Joses. Her husband was "Cleophas" or "Alphaeus." The Gospel of John—which never makes mention of anything like "the Virgin Mary"—agrees that Mary's husband was "Clopas," and by implication that she was the mother of James, Simon, Judas, and Joses. But John is so confused he never even calls Jesus' mother "Mary," but rather "his mother," unnamed—and insists that "Mary" was her sister! Mary was the sister of her own sister Mary.

Robert Eisenman, *Dead Sea Scrolls scholar, professor of Religious Studies at*
California State University at Long Beach, and author of James the Brother of Jesus

We don't know whether she had other children or not for sure. But she certainly was a womanly member of the human species, so clearly she wasn't sexless. She was a woman who was so attractive and so wonderful that God fell in love with her. In a special way.

Father Andrew Greeley, *sociologist and author*

In Mallet, Louisiana, a town of fifty families, they taught us that Mary was the mother of Jesus. When she died she was taken up to heaven, not just her spirit but her body too. She was crowned Queen of Heaven when she made it up there. She was a good example to follow. When the Holy Spirit came down to ask her if she would accept the Conception, that was a bold step in faith, because in that time they would stone you if you were found pregnant and unmarried. And to be the Mother of Christ—to accept that was a bold step. And she just said, "Whatever, make me your handmaiden. Whatever you got to do with me, do with me."

That was a really good example of faith for me. Totally trusting in what God wants you to do.

Terrance Simien, *zydeco recording artist*

This "yes" that she said—"thy will be done"—is such an incredible example to all Christians, it's a "yes" that reverberates in hearts and minds today. The basic question—how must I say yes to God in order that I might do His will?—you just can't get around it. It defines the life of every individual. Mary's yes—how she risked all, and how she so completely trusted in God—that's an ideal I work toward on a daily basis. The most important thing in the life of a human being is to discern what God's will is for you in your life and to do it com-pletely. Then when all is said and done, you must stand before God and say "I have done your will. I have done your will."

Greg Simien, *Terrance's brother, a divinity student who, after being ordained a priest, plans to work for the diocese of Lafayette, Louisiana*

The Growth of Mary

The Mary of today started not with Christ's birth, nor with the Gospels, but with a second-century document called The Book of James. The text filled in details of Mary's birth, marriage, and Annunciation. It was not then—and never has been—accorded canonical authority, but that didn't prevent it from inspiring the tradition of devotion to Our Lady.

But even with James, Mary was barely formed. In the second century the concept of Jesus' virgin birth was fiercely debated, and the notion that Mary remained a virgin her entire life wasn't on the table. By the fifth century, however, Mary's perpetual virginity was part of who she was. The Council of Ephesus in 431 accorded her, against much opposition, the title Mother of God. This boosted Mary toward being, as historian Karen Armstrong puts it, "a major celebrity."

Which meant a figure worth shaping. The Bible offers no other human so useful in this way: extremely significant in the Christ story, yet so inscrutable that she can be known—and used—in various ways through subtle amendment. "Mary is continuously reinvented," says Armstrong, author of A History of God and the recent In the Beginning: A New Interpretation of Genesis. "In each age, people have changed their definition of her to fit their own circumstances." With each new incarnation, however, the old "inventions" do not slip away. They accrue, they pile up.

As an object lesson about how liberal and conservative Christians have put very different spins on Mary, look at the Annunciation— the scene in Luke's Gospel where the angel Gabriel asks Mary if she will bear God's child. Through the years, and still today, those who have required a compliant Mary have seized on the "Behold the

Christ in the Stable, C. Pal Molnar

handmaid of the Lord" phrase and Mary's submissive "Be it unto me according to thy will." By contrast, those who see Mary as an independent woman have pointed out that God didn't force a decision on her, he sent Gabriel to gain her consent. The choice was Mary's. "If by her own free will she had refused God—as Eve did—then the plan had to change," says Pelikan. "The entire plan of salvation hung in the balance. So if, as various interpreters have said, God does not rape, God woos, then it had to be a free and independent source of action in Mary that made this happen. This makes her not a passive receptacle."

One scene, two opposite Marys. This sort of thing has happened time and again, and it was a factor leading to the split in Christianity and the rise of Protestant churches.

In medieval times a metaphysical concept attached itself to Mary, that of the Immaculate Conception—often confused with the virgin birth of Jesus—which held that she was free of Original Sin from her first moment in the womb of her mother, rendering her saintly even before birth. Mary herself is said to have confirmed the doctrine in a fourteenth century visitation to St. Bridget of Sweden, and this added to the growing number of Marys: human; docile and handmaidenly; smart and strong; saintly and capable of supernatural appearances. "She even becomes a military figure," says Pelikan. "She is a warrior against the devil. In Constantinople they went to war with the Virgin on the sails of their warships. Onward Christian soldiers!"

To the degree that Catholicism departed from the simple biblical view of Mary and listed toward a more ethereal Mary, the Protestant Reformation begged to differ with Rome. The reformers—Luther, Calvin, others—saw a good, married, loving mother as an excellent role model. End of story. The Mary of the Immaculate Conception seemed to be claiming spiritual attributes properly reserved for Christ. The Vatican turned a deaf ear to the Reformers, boosting Marian devotion at the Council of Trent (1545–63) and instituting the Feast of the Holy Rosary in 1573. Hail Marys fell like rain, and new prayers to Our Lady were written every day.

Mary, Mother of grace, Mother of mercy,

Shield me from the enemy, and receive me at the hour of my death…

I remember the first time I really wondered about Mary. I was watching "A Charlie Brown Christmas" its first year out, and Linus had finished his speech, which has the angel proclaiming, "'Tis Christ the Lord." I started thinking about the angels that had appeared in the Middle East: Gabriel to Mary, the shepherds' angels. I had never seen one, and as I watched the show I wondered about, and grew troubled by, all these

angels. I had doubt. But then I thought about Christ's heroism and began
to reason backward. If he was that good, then what must she have been?
Maybe she was touched by...

I was still a kid, but this was when I started to come to terms with
faith—as opposed to memorization, and as opposed to mere trust.

Robert Sullivan, LIFE *magazine, December 1996*

And so it was, that, while they were there, the days were accomplished that she should be delivered.

And she brought forth her firstborn son, and wrapped him in swaddling clothes, and laid him in a manger; because there was no room for them at the inn.   Luke 2:6-7

Baby (The Nativity), Paul Gauguin

It is proper to call you blessed, ever-esteemed *Theotokos*, most pure, Mother of God. You who are more worthy of honor than the cherubim and far more glorious than the seraphim. You who incorruptibly gave birth to God the Word, very *Theotokos*, we fervently extol thee.

Ancient Greek prayer

The beauty of Orthodox Christianity is found in its purity, its completeness and its constancy of purpose. Orthodoxy—or "true worship"—is the manifestation of God's love for mankind, expressed most perfectly in the incarnation of His only begotten Son, through the power of the Holy Spirit and through the sublime obedience and humility of the Ever-Virgin Mary—the Theotokos, "Mother of God."

It was through the Theotokos that God made ready a holy throne for Himself upon the Earth and prepared a living heaven in His love for us. Those who embrace the unspoiled beauty of Orthodox Christianity experience both the seen and unseen living heaven on Earth, and drink from the life-giving fountain of salvation that is granted to them upon their death by the Ever-Virgin Mary's son, Jesus Christ, the resurrected Lord and mankind's Savior.

The Ever-Virgin Mary is at the very heart of Orthodoxy's splendor and is the most magnificent embodiment of beauty that has ever blossomed forth from the world, "more honorable than the cherubim and more glorious beyond compare than the seraphim." She is unequivocally linked to our salvation because God chose her from among all women to bear the Son of Man—God incarnate. By her complete acceptance of the will of God in her life, He consecrated her through the life-creating power of the Holy Spirit in a way that has never and will never be experienced by any other human being.

During her life, the Ever-Virgin Mary, the holiest of women, served God with profound obedience, fasting and constant prayer, her appearance ever beautiful and glorious. She was at once human and angelic, and sanctified the earthly world through her embrace of the divine world. As the Theotokos, she is most blessed because

Virgin Mary and Child, unknown

she is the most faithful daughter of God the Father, the Mother of His Incarnate Son and sacred temple of the resplendent Holy Spirit. Indeed, she is the most exalted among God's creatures in her role as most eminent mediator between humanity and Christ.

Since the Ever-Virgin Mary was conceived by marital union, she was therefore burdened like every human being with a weak nature

Virgin and Child, unknown

and the inevitability of physical death. However, she was victorious in her life through the expression of her own free will in obedience to and love for God. As the Theotokos, she was saved by her divine Son—the New Adam, the holy and just one—the first and only child born to her, the New Eve.

The Light—the Holy Spirit—cleansed the Ever-Virgin Mary's mind, her flesh and her nature, and sanctified her virginity, as is so eloquently reflected in the Byzantine Akathist Hymn: "When the great Archangel saw You O Pure One, the living Bible of Christ, sealed by the Spirit, he cried unto You: Hail! O vessel of gladness, through whom the curse of the first mother is loosed." And for each of us, the Theotokos, the Saint of Saints illuminated by God's grace, stands as a vigilant mother, watching over us on Earth and spiritually holding us, like her Son, in her arms forever.

As spoken by the prophets before the Ever-Virgin Mary's birth, then heralded by the Archangel Gabriel in his divine message of her election to bear the Son of the Most High, and culminating in her free acceptance of God's plan, Mary was placed at the center of a most glorious proclamation of truth, peace, hope, and love. This proclamation is the Gospel of salvation offered by God to humanity in Jesus Christ, the Son of the All-Holy Theotokos.

His Eminence Archbishop Spyridon, *primate of the Greek Orthodox Archdiocese of America*

The Eastern Orthodoxy all have magnificent Marian tributes. Roman Catholicism is weak in Marian devotion compared to Eastern Catholics. They don't have the rosary there—it's a Western prayer—but they've got some beautiful hymns, some beautiful icons too.

Father Thomas Thompson, *of the International Marian Research Institute in Dayton, Ohio*

Belief gives me an antenna to a wide range of melodies, and allows them to resonate inside me. My father used to say that while everyone else would say either/or, I would always say both/and. I am drawn to figures and themes that are inclusive and comprehensive—and Mary is one of those figures. Is Mary a figure of humility or of glory? The answer is yes.

Jaroslav Pelikan, *of Yale, author of* Mary Through the Centuries

It is only with the Protevangelium of James in the Second Century, a document put in the name of Jesus' brother, closest living relative and successor, that two claims emerge: One, that Jesus' "brothers" are not real brothers but, rather, half-brothers or step-brothers; and, two, of the "perpetual virginity" of Mary, which in fact rules out that Mary could have had any other children either before or after the birth of Jesus, and that this birth itself was miraculous. This is the doctrine of the Catholic Church as we know it and as it developed, with the slight addition from Jerome in the fourth or fifth century that these were all really "cousins," not brothers.

Robert Eisenman, *Dead Sea Scrolls scholar*

Through Church history, into the Mary figure is poured Isis of Egypt, the Black Madonna, the feminine characteristic of all the mystery religions. My sense is that Mary the Virgin as we have received her in Western civilization is a male construct of what we think women ought to be.

Bishop John Spong, *of Newark, New Jersey, author of* Born of a Woman

As modern scripture scholarship has uncovered the ways in which the Gospels were formed, it has become more and more apparent how little we really know about Mary, and so she is a figure who, like many saints and martyrs in many religious traditions, has been terribly politicized throughout the ages to serve the agendas of various factions.

Andrea M. Johnson, *National Coordinator, Women's Ordination Conference*

Mary is a strong person, a mature adult, an example of courage and perseverance. She was together with Christ in His struggle. I think the view of her as passive came with subsequent historical periods. Under powers that were dominant and colonial, there was a need to present her as submissive to God, emphasizing the male descending from heaven. It is not right to neglect her exile, her drive to keep

Flight into Egypt IV, Gillian Lawson

her baby safe from the killings of Herod. Jesus joined groups against the dictator, and Mary would have been with them. He had meetings in His house, meetings that were rebellious. She was with Him through all this. She suffered with Him throughout the time that He was falsely accused, tortured, condemned to death, and killed. Mary did not run away with the Apostles. She was at the foot of the cross with Him. We can think of Mary as the backbone of the early Church, yet these things are now neglected. We need to change our image of her. Mary is full of grace, she is the model for peace and humanity. But a few officials in Sri Lanka and the Vatican say I am diluting Mary. I say this is not true.

Father Tissa Balasuriya, *author of* Mary and Human Liberation *and a Roman Catholic priest from Sri Lanka who is appealing his recent excommunication, which resulted, in part, from a dispute over whether the Vatican has the authority to deny women the priesthood*

The Madonna of Loreto, Sanzio Raphael of Urbino

A fascinating connection between the Virgin Mary and Native American beliefs: When the Spanish came to the New World, they brought with them the idea that blue was a sacred color, and also that it was the color of the Virgin Mary. In Mexico, they found that a number of Indian tribes already considered blue a sacred color that protected people from harm. This helped priests persuade native

Madonna and Child with Angels, Mark Lancelot Symons

peoples of the sacredness of the Virgin Mary—she wore blue, blue was a sacred color, ergo she herself was sacred and could protect from harm. The same was true not only in Mexico but in what is now New Mexico and Arizona. Today around Santa Fe, where I live, there is still a strong folk belief in the power of the color turquoise, in all its shades, to protect from evil. Doors and window sills have long been painted turquoise as a way of protecting a home against evil. Anglo newcomers have adopted the custom not as a religious belief but as a fashion statement.

Susan Hazen-Hammond, *author of* Timelines of Native American History

My favorite Mary story goes like this: Mother Teresa, God bless her, finally passes on and goes—of course—straight to heaven, where she is warmly greeted by Saint Peter. Peter tells her she can pick her wish. Her life has been such a blessing to those on earth, she can have whatever she wants in heaven. Teresa, delighted, asks to have lunch with Mary, the Blessed Mother, and Peter arranges for the best table in the house. The women sit down, talk for hours, really get to know each other. Finally Teresa ask the question she has always longed to ask. "Why, Mary, do you always look slightly—ever so slightly—sad in all the beautiful images we have of you? Even now, you have a certain sadness in your eyes, even as we speak of wondrous and glorious things. Tell me, Mother Mary, what is it?"

Mary says, "Teresa, you are as insightful as everyone has said you are. Yes, there is a small, small sadness in my life."

"Well, what could it be, Blessed Mother?" asks Teresa.

Mary sighs. "I was actually hoping for a girl."

Regina Barreca, *professor of Gender and Literature at the University of Connecticut, Storrs, Connecticut, author of* They Used to Call Me Snow White...But I Drifted: Women's Strategic Uses of Humor, *and editor of* The Penguin Book of Women's Humor

I don't see why we shouldn't continuously reinvent Mary. I do like her original image: that of everything the sacred Christian should be. But maybe we shouldn't be tied to just one image of Mary. If the peasant Mary is what does it for you, run with it. But if you're moved by the thought of her at the right hand of the Father, up there with the greats, so to speak, in a great union of the male and female elements—well, go with that.

Karen Armstrong, *author of* A History of God

The Dogma of Mary

During the past 150 years, the Vatican has issued three new dogmas, and two have concerned Mary: first, absolute belief in the Immaculate Conception, and second, absolute belief in the Assumption—Mary's bodily rise to heaven. Both upset the Protestants mightily, but what could they do?

Well, they could appeal to the more liberal of the Catholic clergy, which they did. At the seminal Catholic congress of the modern age—the Second Vatican Council (1962–65)—one of the most dramatic debates concerned Mary: How otherworldly is she? Liberal Catholic bishops tried, in the candid assessment of *Inside the Vatican* magazine, "to speak little about Mary, to 'downplay' her role," so as to forward the march toward a reunification of Christian churches—toward ecumenism. After months of holy war, liberals carried the day—by a margin of seventeen after 2,100 bishops had cast ballots. In some U.S. churchyards, statues of Mary were removed from their pedestals.

But never count the Marians out. The pendulum swung back in 1969 when Pope Paul VI lifted a canonical requirement that religious books, including ones on apparitions, be preapproved. In 1974 he sought, in the words of feminist theologian Marina Warner, "to represent her as the steely champion of the oppressed and a woman of action and resolve." This sounded good to many modernist women in the Church, who wondered if a new day was dawning for them. *Inside the Vatican*, commenting on the "remarkable and completely unexpected rebirth of attention" to Mary, said the aims of Vatican II had been foiled "by events themselves, as if a 'higher authority'

Repose in Egypt, Sir Edward Burne-Jones

has decreed that Mary receive great honor despite all the hesitations of 'reasonable' theologians."

Pope John Paul II has been the leader of the world's Catholics since 1978. He has also been the standard-bearer for the world's classical Marians. This Polish Pope's view of the Virgin is so traditional it has caused concern within the Church. In a 1994 address to 150 young priests, Cardinal Carlo Maria Martini, sometimes mentioned as successor to John Paul, confronted these qualms: "There has been an unspoken sense that Marian devotion is necessarily 'popular,' that is, only for the common people. For example, faced with the warmth and intensity of John Paul II's dedication to Mary, this elite reacts by attributing the Pope's fervor to 'national characteristics,' a 'more emotional' sensitivity....I believe the time has come to take a new look at the state of Marian devotion, to find an equilibrium between theological clarity and the spiritual yearnings of the Christian people and of ourselves. Otherwise, we may face a dangerous loss of warmth and feeling in our faith, our prayer, and our life....We have arrived at a point where this cold, scientific attitude no longer responds to an obvious emotional need for an attachment to Mary."

It still seems to some that the sentimental side of the Pope's Marian devotion outweighs the objective. His motto is *Totus tuus* ("All yours"— referring to Mary). When he survived the would-be assassin Mehmet Ali Agca's bullets on May 13, 1981, he noted that the attack occurred on the anniversary of the 1917 Church-approved apparition at Fatima, Portugal, and he credited his survival to intercession by the Blessed Virgin. When godless communism fell in the Eastern bloc, which included his beleaguered homeland, the Pope said this, too, was thanks to Mary.

That the Pope loves Mary, no one questions. But the way the Pope employs Mary defines every ongoing Mary debate and leaves feminist theologians, many Protestants, and some Catholics frustrated or furious. "He visits Mary shrines but says women can't be priests," says Father Andrew Greeley, the sociologist and novelist from Chicago. "He's an Eastern European romantic intellectual. They operate under different logical rules than North American persons like me."

Immaculate Mary, you appeared to St. Bernadette

And gave her a mission to build up Lourdes

As a sacred shrine to bring people to God...

My grandmother, who was French American, used to tell me about Lourdes. I could sense she had trouble with it. She was a small, loving, practical woman; I don't think she ever willfully told a lie. So the Lourdes story came out not as history but as fantasy. As I remember it, the Bernadette she told me about was Hollywood's Jennifer Jones version. I loved the story, but loved it as a story—the way I loved The Wizard of Oz.

The Virgin, Abbott Handerson Thayer

When my grandmother had finished the tale, we would say a rosary together. As we did, it was as if the Mary of the rosary was an entirely other Mary than the one who had appeared, in 1858, to fourteen-year-old Bernadette Soubirous. The Lourdes Mary made for a nice story. The other we believed in.

Then, years later, I learned that my Church said everything my grandmother had told me about Lourdes was true.

Faith is often hard, but that's no secret.

Robert Sullivan, LIFE *magazine, December 1996*

The human Mary of the Gospels has been lost in man's attempt to make her something she was not. Mary was a woman. She lived her life. She died and went to meet her Son in heaven. Mary was what she was. Those using her to further their own agendas should be careful.

Patricia Pfeiffer, *author of the novel*
Above All Women: The Story of the Virgin Mary

I lost my chair because I doubted the Virgin Birth. The Virgin Birth—I believed it, said it in my lectures. But then I didn't—it took me seventeen years to come to this disbelief. I questioned the Virgin Birth in 1987. Ever since then, at the school, they still mention that Professor Ranke Heinemann is doing a lecture but they always mention that the lecture is not authorized by the Catholic Church. For when it comes to the Virgin Birth, you can't be a Catholic if you don't believe.

When I lost my chair, there was quite a fuss in the newspapers. One person asked me, "I don't understand. Whether Mary is a virgin, the question is not so important." And it struck me, that's true. For Protestants, this question is not at all important. But it is the very essence of Catholic theology. Because as soon as you say Mary was not a virgin, the whole system collapses.

Uta Ranke Heinemann, *first woman in the world to hold a chair of Catholic Theology—at the University of Essen—and the first woman in the world to lose such a chair*

These three ideas about Mary are the ones I think about, and that seem to work for me.

The first is to stress Mary biblically. This represents the developing faith of the earliest Christians, and leads to the second point—Mary as the first disciple and first believer. Mary is the first to hear the word. She "ponders these things in her heart." The words suggest the need to think about things that are profound over a long period of time, a lifetime. For modern Christians, for whom faith is a struggle and questions are constant, Mary is a model of one who asks hard questions, has second thoughts, and leaves answers on hold, pondering them over a long time.

The third idea is Mary and social justice, and the struggle for freedom. It is significant how different Mariology is in the developing and developed world. Mary in Latin and Central America is not the same as here in the Northeast. Brazilian theologian Clodovis Boff says that one community in the Amazon jungle wondered what Mary meant to them when her words said that God has confused the mighty and lifted the lowly, fed the hungry with every good thing and sent the rich away empty. Mary, it seemed to them, was like a person in their own experience, a "matiero," a person who hacks a path for others to follow, through the jungle, with a machete.

Father Robert Bullock, *Rector of Our Lady of Sorrows, Sharon, Massachusetts*

The Youth of our Lord, John Rogers Herbert

The dogma of the Assumption means that Mary is in heaven with the other saints. What was said about Mary in terms of "the Assumption" actually applies to all saints, it's just that the Pope singled out Mary. For all saints, there's a resurrection of the body in some spiritual sense—the whole person is brought into eternal happiness.

She's at the right hand of the Father only in the sense that everyone is at the right hand of the Father. That is, all saints are in the company of the Father, but none is equal to Jesus. He's the Son of the Father and co-equal. This doesn't mean anything more than the fact that Mary is joining the company of saints. She can be called the preeminent saint in the communion of saints, but obviously no saint including Mary is equal to Jesus. The risen Christ is exalted and sits at the right hand of the Father in a position of equality. No one else sits there except Christ.

Father Richard McBrien, *professor of Religion at Notre Dame University in South Bend, Indiana, and author of* Catholicism

The Catholic Church has never called Mary an Apostle, but it calls her a lot more than that. That's rather a puny status compared to what she is, given her Assumption into heaven, the fact that she's the only one born without Original Sin, that she's the Mother of God. The title "Apostle" would be rather trivial.

Jaroslav Pelikan, *of Yale, author of* Mary Through the Centuries

As a zydeco musician, I'm on the road. I say my rosary. I can say any prayer, but I'll say my rosary, and I'll get a peaceful feeling. I do it at different times. Sometimes in the morning. Sometimes I'll be in the van doing nothing and I'll say a rosary. Sometimes I get scared, or start to missing home, and say a rosary. Or start to worrying about someone back home, and say a rosary. I'm asking her to pray with me to God.

Terrance Simien, *zydeco recording artist*

Miraculous Mary

There are a thousand and one Marys at work in the world today, but there's something more than mere convenience to the argument that after two thousand years we are delivered four principal Marys who seek to soothe the soul of modern man. Each is unique, each powerful in her way.

The one most powerful in supernatural ways is Miraculous Mary.

In January 1993, retired bread-truck driver Ray Doiron, 58, was getting ready for bed in Renault, Illinois. A lovely woman appeared to him, "a very beautiful lady, very young and regal. She was dressed all in white." He felt a breeze and heard her speak. She delivered the first of many messages—"pray for peace," "reject evil," "welcome God"—that she would continue to offer in subsequent visitations.

"I come to you as a loving mother," she said. Doiron, a humble man, wondered, Why me? She said: "I picked you because you are the least apt instrument. Therefore, people that know you will know this is not your word."

Doiron had already been, for twenty years, a regular visitor to Our Lady of the Snows shrine over in Belleville. After experiencing this initial vision at home, he began to be visited at the shrine. People heard about this, and soon the crowds grew too great for the shrine's Lourdes Grotto. Today, pilgrims begin arriving at nine A.M. at a nearby amphitheater to get the best seats.

Father William Clark, director of the shrine, says carefully, "I can't claim what he does or doesn't see." But he is not entirely dismissive: "I'll tell you what I see. I see six thousand people coming to pray, which is a very good thing."

4:30 AM Christmas Morning, Christopher Lauber

In Bayside, Queens, New York, where there was a Mary appearance in 1970, a brochure of her wisdom can be obtained by calling a toll-free number—1-800-345-MARY. In Italy, fifty weeping Madonna statues have been reported in the past two years. Across the world, countless Polaroids purport to show the Virgin. "Some of the apparition stuff approaches the bizarre," says Jaroslav Pelikan.

Virgin Mary San Xavier Del Bac, unknown

Theologians and even Catholic clergy are decidedly uneasy about the sightings. "Sure, there's no doubt that the apparitions have multiplied," says Father Thomas Thompson of the International Marian Research Institute in Dayton, "but I think it has a lot to do with the Medjugorje thing, which has still received no approval."

The Medjugorje thing: In 1981, six young peasants reported a visit by the Virgin in Eastern Europe. She has been delivering messages to them and others almost nightly ever since, attracting no fewer than eleven million believers to Medjugorje. As he watched the flock flock in earlier this decade, Pavao Zanic, retired Bishop of Mostar, grew apoplectic. "The Madonna has never said anything at Medjugorje," declared Zanic, who is appalled at seeing Mary turned into "a tourist attraction." Father Castellano Cervera, a specialist in Mariology who is consulting with the Vatican as it looks into such situations, understands Zanic's anger, but says, "It seems clear to me that one can go to Medjugorje, just as one goes to any sanctuary, to deepen one's Christian life."

Father Cervera sees the pilgrims not as lookers but seekers. Others agree. "Church leaders must ask serious questions," says Donna Orsuto of the Foyer Unitas Institute in Rome, a theological think tank. "Why are so many flocking to these places of visions and signs? What are they seeking that they are not finding through normal channels of Marian devotion in the Church?"

LIFE *magazine, December 1996*

Two workmen are busy repainting the ceiling of the local church, putting finishing touches on the clouds and on the stars that have been in place for a hundred years. They're up on the scaffolding, working away, when a little old lady from the village walks in. Her head bowed, she's dressed in black and her rosary is already out. One guy whispers to the other, "Let's have a little fun with Grandma down there." He lowers his voice and says from his position in the sky, "This is the Lord. What have you come to ask me?"

The little old lady just walks over to the pew, kneels, crosses herself, and begins to pray. She doesn't even look up. "She must be hard of hearing, the old dear," says the other workman. So the first one does his routine again, only more loudly.

"This is the Lord. What have you come to ask me?"

There's no response this time, either. She continues to pray.

"Come on, Jack, give it one more go," suggests the other painter. The first one, even more loudly this time, yells, "This is the Lord! What have you come to ask me?"

The little old lady finally looks up and yells back impatiently, "Will you just be quiet for a minute? I'm busy talking to your mother!"

Regina Barreca, *editor of* The Penguin Book of Women's Humor

As for visions, I don't doubt them. I may doubt if they are really seeing Mary. Why doesn't she just appear—like the prophet Samuel—rather than in a misty vision? However, I do not doubt the faith of those who have seen her over the centuries. If it increases their faith, so be it. There is danger, though, because the visions are more tangible than God. People may trust the appearance instead of the Creator. These visions may not diminish Mary, but they do cloud the real person she was and is.

Patricia Pfeiffer, *author of the novel* Above All Women: The Story of the Virgin Mary

The Vatican rarely gives attention to the apparitions. There's no doubt that Marian apparitions have multiplied—this may be partly due to the fact that formerly such things, by canon law, were forbidden to be discussed. Maybe it's just like the interest in the angels. It could be a desire for some breakthrough to the supernatural. Perhaps religion has become a little too intellectual, cerebral, academic. Another thing is that apparitions provide certitude, surety. There's always that desire in religion.

It's a very deep question: Do miracles lead people to deep faith, or do they stop at the apparition?

Father Thomas Thompson, *of the International Marian Research Institute*

I made a trip to Medjugorge in April 1991. I went as a journalist, but also as a wobbly Catholic, who, although balanced near the end of belief, still believed that Mary could *do* it, if I called upon her with true heart. And I wanted her to do something, very much—I wanted her to do something for me this time, and my wife: I wanted her to give us life. For years, we had been trying to have a baby, and—as I always answered at that time, when the well-meaning asked if my wife and I had any children—we still hadn't been "blessed" in that regard, and so I went to Medjugorge not only to write a story but to ask for Mary's blessing. I mean, why not? I mean, that's what she *does*, right? She is blessed, so she gives blessings, even to those of us mired in skepticism, even to those of us not only faithless but determinedly so, even to those for whom belief in Mary is a vestige of something else, some earlier day, and hence the belief we are most afraid to lose. I was superstitious, in other words, in regard to the Virgin. On the evening of my thirty-third birthday, I met up with a group of pilgrims— people call themselves pilgrims, rather than tourists, when they go to Medjugorge—at Kennedy Airport, and when they began their incessant chanting of the Rosary, I forced myself to join in, even though I hadn't said the Rosary in something like fifteen years, and had forgotten some of the more esoteric creeds. They were the subjects of my story, these pilgrims, and so, of course, I wanted to understand them, I wanted to ingratiate myself with them, I wanted to *fool* them, but more than that, I couldn't imagine not saying the Hail Mary, when—once we got on the plane, and flew to what was then called Yugoslavia—all I *heard* was the Hail Mary, in at least ten different languages, for ten days. The Hail Mary, you see, is not a prayer to abjure. It is—was—a prayer I *had* to say, to fool the pilgrims, to fool myself, to fool *her*, and once I made myself say it it I didn't *stop* saying it, and for ten days its words bent and shaped my lips.

I didn't like Medjugorge, by the way. The place, I mean; the *location*—I didn't like it, because although it had its share of beauty, and its very sunlight had the power to proselytize, it was a jagged place, and its mountains and hills looked like slag heaps, and when you fell to your knees in prayer, you stood up pierced and bleeding. I saw a lot of bleeding knees, in Medjugorge. I guess that's because

Madonna doll, dressed for different occasions, Portuguese folk art

I saw a lot of people on their knees, greedy for miracles of light and, of course, of luck. I mean, there was a kind of masochism at work in Medjugorge—the kind of Catholicism that makes a fetish of suffering both human and divine—and after a while the very ground seemed kind of...I don't know...*bloodthirsty*, or something. I saw so much suffering there, so much desperate entreaty, so many bent and broken believers dispensing themselves from their wheelchairs in order to wiggle like worms up sharp rocks, that after a while it was not the capture of affliction, but rather the promise of relief, that seemed, in itself, a kind of cruelty. In the course of my ten days there, I wound up focusing more and more on a woman, Carol Leland, who was desperately ill, who was in a wheelchair and dependent on a bullet-shaped tank of oxygen for breath, and who almost died, in search of some kind of blessing. Of course, the thing with Carol is that she shouldn't have *been* there, in Medjugorge, at all, but there she was, and her gasping quest—spiritual, physical—was at once magnificent and obliquely suicidal. "Lord, I am not worthy to receive you," Catholics say, before they ingest God's host, "but only say the word, and I shall be healed." Well, in Medjugorge, there was a massed and astonishing hunger for the word, *that* word, the magic word that is at once implicitly promised and implicitly denied—forever on the tip of the divine tongue—and at night, when the famished pilgrims marched into the barbed mountains to garner their messages from Mary, I clung close to Carol, to find out if she ever heard what she needed to hear, and to find out, for myself, what in the world that might be.

I didn't hear it, myself. The word: I didn't hear it, and so, of course, I didn't *get* it—I wasn't healed. I prayed, but I wasn't *convinced*. I didn't start the trip believing, and I didn't end the trip believing. And as for my own grovelling prayers: they didn't work, of course—not this time. My sneaky chorus of whispered praise, my disingenuous volley of Hail Marys—She just didn't buy it, I guess. She didn't buy it, and neither did He, or They, and my wife and I were not blessed with children then, and we are not blessed with children now. That's not to say that I got *rooked*, or something, in Medjugorge; that's not to say that I didn't get my money's worth—indeed, I saw what so many of the pilgrims came to see. I saw a miracle, on one of my last days there. Toward sunset, I went alone to the west side of the big church, and there I saw hundreds of pilgrims staring gaspingly at the sun, in the belief that it had started to spin. The Miracle of the Sun, this is called—and I *saw* it, by God. No, I don't think the sun was spinning, exactly; but you could look at it, and you didn't have to worry about burning your eyes. These were the last days of Yugoslavia; the last days before the secession of Croatia; the last days before the raw bloody birth of Bosnia; the last days before the massacres; the last days before the ethnic cleansings…and now at the last of this day there was a sun in the sky shorn of its barbed heat, and recast as an emblem of mercy. It was a sun that *invited* you to look at it: an acid-trippy sun, a sun that seemed to pulse with pity—a *personal* sun, just as the Christian God is said to be a personal God. I did not gasp, however, and I did not fall to my knees, and I did not renew my old pledge of fealty to Mary. I had asked her for a miracle, and although she had given me one, it wasn't the miracle I wanted, and it wasn't miracle enough.

Tom Junod, *Writer at Large,* Esquire *magazine*

The exact date of Our Lady of Guadalupe's appearance to Juan Diego is December 12, 1531. Today on December 12, people around the Americas honor Our Lady of Guadalupe. They dance the *Matachines,* a winter dance—an ancient dance that combines Spanish and Indian motifs. For Catholics, Our Lady of Guadalupe is the patron of the Americas. At her core, she is primarily a religious figure who merges Catholic and Aztec traditions, but her significance extends far beyond religion into such areas as politics, history, folk history, social justice, humanistic psychology, and feminism.

Susan Hazen-Hammond, *author of* Timelines of Native American History

In 1986 I found myself at a low point in my life. I'd married the year before and thought that this would be all that I needed in order to be happy, content, and set for life—especially since I'd found a wonderful mate. But at the time, I was suffering from a yet undiagnosed case of agoraphobia, with severe panic attacks and depression. I prayed for answers as I had been taught to pray as a Methodist and later in Southern Baptist churches.

One day I was in a bookstore looking for more information. I was praying that God would guide me to the place I could receive this information, whether it was a church, books, or a person. A book fell off the shelf. I replaced it. Another book fell off the shelf, and once again I picked the book up and replaced it. The clerk said to me,

Crucifixion, Tommaso Masaccio

"I think that book is trying to get your attention." It was the same book as before—*The God–Mind Connection*. Toward the back of the book there was information about spirit guides who called themselves The Brotherhood of God, and identified themselves as an outreach of the Holy Spirit. They gave vague instructions on how to contact them and receive messages.

After several months of receiving daily messages from The Brotherhood of God, I began to feel a presence in my house. A few days later, I felt

Compianto sul Cristo morto, Sandro Botticelli

the presence again and smelled the overwhelming aroma of something very sweet. The sweet smell was of roses, and an indication that Mary was present. A few days later, I began to hear my name being called. I thought it was a voice outside me. But now I know that no one else can hear it. I used to say I heard it in my mind, but it's more than my mind. I hear her voice throughout my whole being.

She said she had a message to send to the world and she wanted to send it through me. I was terrified. She convinced me that she had chosen me for this task. I agreed to take the message down. It took over two years to receive the message that became my book. It was given in daily lessons. She asked me to live the message to the best of my ability. She said that we need to learn to love ourselves. She urges us all to cleanse our hearts of anger and fear.

Annie Kirkwood, *author of* Mary's Message to the World
and co-editor of Mary's Message/Newsletter

Mediator Mary

Father Andrew Greeley, the noted sociologist from Chicago, relates one of his favorites: "Once upon a time, the Lord went walking through the streets of heaven, and He saw a lot of people who had no business being in heaven at all. So the Lord goes to the Gates of Heaven, where St. Peter sits at his laptop. He says, 'Simon Peter, you've let me down! There are people with no business being here, and you let them in!' 'Boss, it's not my fault.' 'Well,' says the Lord, 'Who let them in?' 'I don't want to tell ye, because ye'll be angry,' says Peter. 'Ye better tell me, I'm the boss!' 'Well,' says Peter, 'all right, but ye won't like it. I tell them folks they can't get in, and don't they go around to the back door, and your mother lets them in?!'

"That's the whole idea behind Mary, I think."

Heaven always sounds like a suburb of Dublin when Greeley's telling the jokes. But the point is valid. Mary's role as intercessor and ally is certainly the largest part in the Story of Mary. Why? Because in a world asked to be God-fearing, humankind requires someone or something to help us fight the fear.

"Saint Bernard had a sermon in which he portrayed not only God but also Christ as judges of the quick and the dead," says Jaroslav Pelikan. "And then Bernard says, 'Therefore you should hide behind Mary, who by showing her breast to Christ reminds him of where he received his life.' She mitigates divine wrath."

The more wrathful heaven seems, the more a mediator is needed for those who would preserve their faith. And it's never easy to go directly to the one you are blaming or to the one you fear. "When TWA Flight 800 went down, people were asking, 'How can God allow

Assumption of the Virgin, Anonymous

such a thing?'" says Forrest Church, pastor of the Unitarian All Souls Church in New York City. "But then they'd turn around and pray for the victims, and many would pray to Mary. She, they could pray to—for support and nurturing. And I mean nurturing in a strong, not a weak, way. She would put their tough questions to God on their behalf. She would lift them up and help them move forward." And these are Unitarians.

Holy Mother Mary,

I place myself under your loving protection

And ask the help of your intercession…

We were taught that we could pray for ourselves, but not for material things. We were told that we had options: God would listen, Jesus would

listen, Mary would listen. My habit, as an adolescent, was to pray to
Jesus. I was a boy; he had been a boy. I figured he would understand me
better. I thought he would forgive me when I tried to slip a selfish-boy
request in, like a September win for the Red Sox. To Mary, such a thing
would take some explaining.

Later, the pleas grew more consequential. Life decisions—career changes,
marriage—led to appeals for blessings and guidance; a family member
developed a cancer, and lunchtime novenas at St. Pat's were squeezed
into the day. I found myself praying to Mary.

Something in my training? About motherhood?

Something about intercession, certainly.

Something about Mary.

Jaroslav Pelikan is asked what he considers the most beautiful
description of Mary. "Dante's," he says. "The closing cantos of *The
Divine Comedy.*"

There we find this portrait:

Look now upon the face that is most like

the face of Christ, for only through its brightness

can you prepare your vision to see Him.

Today people look at that face, and see not just the intercessor,
but so many different things.

Robert Sullivan, LIFE *magazine, December 1996*

Thus in every danger thou canst find a refuge in this same glorious
Virgin.   **St. Thomas Aquinas,** *thirteenth century*

The small pockets of Protestant believers both before and after the
Reformation believed that the only mediator between God and
themselves was Christ Jesus. Protestants have ignored Mary to their
loss for fear she would become an object of worship. Consequently,

they don't really know her or give her the place she deserves as the Mother of Jesus.

Patricia Pfeiffer, *author of the novel* Above All Women: The Story of the Virgin Mary, *and a congregant at a Protestant community church in Washington state*

Unwed mother, mother of a kid who couldn't figure out his vocational direction until later than most of his peers, a woman who could figure out how to be a mother and a virgin at the same time: the idea of Mary embodies a number of conflicts and difficulties of ordinary women, and for that she is called upon by ordinary people, by motherless daughters, by women who need to be heard by someone they believe will listen without passing judgment.

Regina Barreca, *of the University of Connecticut*

Mother Mary said she is appearing in the world today as God's agent. She said as God's agent she is reminding us that God is not only masculine, but is also what we consider feminine. He is loving, nurturing, gentle, caring, all the things we think of as feminine. He is also strong, steadfast, and all the things we think of as masculine.

Annie Kirkwood, *author of* Mary's Message to the World

Hail, Mary, full of grace, the Lord is with thee. Hail, hope of the needy, Mother of those who no longer possess a mother. O Mary, when my broken heart moans and is filled with sorrow, when my soul is enveloped in sadness and fear, when the wind of temptation blows, when stormy passions break loose in my soul, when my sins have closed the gates of heaven against me and robbed me of the friendship of my God, in this hour of tribulation and anguish, to whom should I have recourse but to thee, O blessed Mary, consoler of the afflicted and refuge of sinners?

Thomas à Kempis, *1380–1471*

The Assumption of the Virgin, Nicolas Poussin

I was always one of those Catholic kids who preferred the Mother over the Father. A Freudian confession, perhaps, but really, it's just *easier* to love Mary, when you grow up Catholic—because you don't have to. You don't have to believe in her, the way you have to believe in God the Father and Jesus Christ—you don't have to believe in her, for fear of facing the fires of hell. I mean, no one *scares* you into believing in Mary, or into loving her—you just do, and so your belief and your love seem to clarify the whole essence of faith as something voluntary and freely given, as a reflection of some essential human *willingness*, as the fiction that you feel. I was willing to believe in Mary, because I *felt* her, when I prayed to her, in a way that I never felt any ranking member of the Trinity, or even any of the Saints. Of course, I'm hardly alone in this: people *like* saying the Hail Mary, and that's why when you say the Rosary you get to say ten Hail Marys for every Our Father. You say the Our Father, or, as Protestants call it, The Lord's Prayer, and you feel like you're checking in, like you're punching a clock. You say the Hail Mary, and you really feel like you're *praying*—you feel at once like a correspondent in some privileged intimacy, whispering promises in the dark, and like a child, whose only wish is to be cosmically coddled.

Not that I was completely devoid of self-interest in my relationship with Mary, mind you—I don't think anyone is. Indeed, that's one of the reasons you pray to her, that's part of the *deal*: she's a soft touch. You want a boost in your allowance, you don't appeal to your father, who is busy all the time, and notoriously grumpy, to boot; you ask your mother. She gets results. She's got juice, influence—she knows *when* to ask. I was so confident, in fact, of Mary's ability to *get* stuff, that I told myself not to ask her for anything, unless I really needed it—and one time I did. It was 1970, or thereabouts. I was twelve, and my brother, who is ten years older than me—and who was, and is, something of an idol for me—had become eligible not only for the draft, but for something the United States government had instituted to restore some sort of equity to the selection of young men as agents of Indochinese slaughter: the draft lottery. It worked

Coronation of the Virgin, Fra Filippo Lippi

just like those big lotto jackpots—it was on television, and everything—but instead of winning $20 million and being able to quit your job at the post office, you won the opportunity to do a tour in Vietnam. Anyway, I did not want my brother to go to Vietnam. Indeed, in a fit of spiritual pride, I swore that I would not *let* him go to Vietnam—that I would take it upon myself to win God's intercession for him, in this scrimmage of brute fortune—and so the night of the lottery, when my mother and father went downstairs to watch the show, I repaired to my bedroom, and prayed to Mary. I mean, that was my *choice*, to say the Hail Mary, when it really counted, instead of saying the Our Father—because I knew that the Hail Mary was the prayer that really *worked*, and because this, my belief in the Virgin as an instrument of God's mercy, was my last and true faith. I don't even know exactly how many Hail Marys I said that night—although, of course, I tried to count them, as we Catholics were taught to do. I just know that I said one, and never stopped, and kept my eyes squeezed shut for *hours*. I just know that I spent the entire night on my knees, praying with a gambler's bitter fervor, and that when my mother came upstairs, and told me that my brother's birth date was the 343rd number picked, out of 365—that my brother shared the jackpot of the spared—I imagined that I said precisely 343 Hail Marys. I had lost count—all I knew was that I was *somewhere* in the 300s—but I imagined that I had made precisely 343 murmured appeals to the Virgin, and to this day no one can tell me different; to this day, I believe that the Mother of Our Lord listened to me—to me—and that, although powerless in her own right, she succeeded that night in bending the ear and the will of either her all-powerful Son, or His all-powerful Father, who, strangely enough, is not her all-powerful Husband, but simply the source of salvation's seed, the ravishing Swan to Mary's Leda, the Paracletic perpetrator of history's one essential quickie.

Tom Junod, *Writer at Large,* Esquire *magazine*

I was an altar boy at Saint Ann's in our little town of Mallet. Saint Ann was Mary's mother, and the patron saint of Mallet's parish. There was a statue of Mary on the altar of our church. Our Mary was the white Mary—I noticed that she was a white Mary, but her color had nothing to do with what I was praying for.

People would never pray to Mary. We would always pray *with* Mary. "Holy Mary, Mother of God, pray for us sinners, now and at the moment of our death"—we are asking Mary to pray *with* us, just like you'd call up a friend on the phone and say, "Hey, man, I need you to pray for me." We'd get on our knees and ask her to pray with us— we'd pray to God together. I'd ask her to say some prayers for me. Mary, as the Mother of Jesus, the Son of God—if *she's* saying a prayer for you, then, hell, that should be a plus right there.

I'm guessing, of course. No one really knows. That's what faith is all about. That's where that word faith comes in.

Terrance Simien, *zydeco recording artist*

When you talk about Creole culture, you're talking about very Catholic areas. If you look at the Creole culture and you think of the reverence that people have for women and especially their mothers, the Blessed Mother is the perfect paradigm, the ideal of the way that you should relate to mother, or sister or other women members of your family. The Blessed Mother is looked upon as an advocate, as one with a true sense of motherhood, as one who can be of service to everyone who might have a problem or needs comfort at any given moment.

Greg Simien, *divinity student*

Let your protection smother
human turmoil

Dante Gabriel Rossetti, *1828–1882, in the* Paradiso

Modern Mary

As the Bible's most famous woman by a mile, Mary has become a symbolic player in the fight for the ordination of women—particularly in the United States, where male-hierarchical institutions, governmental or religious, can seem antidemocratic, autocratic, wholly unreasonable. But Pope John Paul II, a deeply contemplative man despite what his detractors say, remains resolute. In 1994 he reaffirmed that women would still be denied the pulpit, never mind that Anglican and Episcopal churches were ordaining women.

In a few instances, Catholics have defied the pontiff while attempting to remain members of the Church. On Ash Wednesday, 1996, six Catholic women stood on the steps of St. Matthew's Cathedral in Washington, D.C., and made the sign of the cross on a hundred supporters' foreheads with ashes from burned copies of a Vatican statement declaring the pope's position "infallible." Not long after, a bishop in Germany's Old Catholic church—whose priests are considered authentic but illicit by the Vatican—laid hands on two formerly Roman Catholic women, naming them priests.

The Church's longtime rationale for a males-only priesthood goes like this: Way back then, Mary herself was not a priest, and no women were chosen by Christ as Apostles. Therefore the Church is imitating Christ, and thus doing God's will. Liberal Catholics say that Christ wasn't in the business of naming priests, that there were no Christian priests at all until the third century and that there is evidence of women being ordained in the fifth century. As for the Apostles: They all deserted Christ on the eve of his crucifixion, didn't they? By contrast, Christ's female followers, exemplified by the strong and stalwart Mary Magdalene, were with him till the end.

The Holy Family, Jerry Dienes

Despite the pope's intransigence, the fight is having an effect. The ability of the Church to define women's roles is changing, asserts Father Richard McBrien, professor of religion at Notre Dame and author of *Catholicism.* The outspoken McBrien contends that the all-male, celibate priesthood has become a "dead letter" issue that is "going to collapse soon. The culture is stronger than theology."

The American culture may be demanding change, but other cultures are demanding adherence to tradition, and this has created an interesting, dangerous Marian dynamic: the clash of old and new Marys. "In the United States, this leads to problems," says Dr. Odette Alarcon,

Planchando, Pensando, J. Michael Walker

a psychiatrist at the Center for Research on Women at Wellesley
College in Massachusetts. She has treated many Latin American
female immigrants who have a deep sense of *marianismo,* a cultural
tenet that views the Virgin as a self-sacrificing, passive, chaste feminine ideal. "Mary is pure, beautiful, white—interestingly—and a

mother. Women come here with that tradition and suffer tremendous pain. They want to be liberated but are trapped in their old culture."

Blamed for psychosocial malaises, enlisted in all manner of twentieth century crusade—"Look down, O Mother, upon the vast numbers of babies not allowed to be born," says the pope—Mary gets trapped too. She gets lost. In some instances she seems a brutally hard-edged symbol, light-years from the original.

LIFE *magazine, December 1996*

She is this kind of complex symbol that represents the position of women in the Church, and it's something that a lot of feminists have to struggle with—what to do with that symbolism. She is traditionally held out as the model for women's behavior, and Catholic women have been asked to emulate her. But the issue is that we don't really know anything about Mary, and all that we know is projected on to her by the Catholic Church and its leaders and a lot of the time she is projected into images to keep women in a particular position socially.

A really good example is that picture from a 1950s civics book that was used in Chicago Catholic schools—Mary wearing a halo, and carrying a broom. The caption that goes along with it says that Mary glorified domestic work for women for all time. Here she is exalted with a halo around her head but she's got this broom in her hand. Now, there's nothing in the Bible that says she did domestic work. But the Church projects that onto her and women are supposed to emulate that.

Maurice Hamington, *of Mount St. Mary's College*

Some people see Mary as linked to the issue of the ordination of women. In the mind of the pope, though, it's a separate issue. The pope says there are other dignities besides the priesthood. He has been trying to tell women there's a great sense of dignity, a great sense of completion, without the priesthood. Rather than being antidemocratic, he insists there are differences between men and women, and separate

Morning Devotions, Rick Beerhorst

dignities. The dignity of bearing children, for instance. Of course, some feminists object to that as a dignity, but the dignity of women bearing children is a dignity to be appreciated.

People will keep agitating for women in the priesthood, and there's no doubt a lot of women have left and been ordained Protestant ministers. But many people feel the ordination of women is just not going to happen for a very, very long time, if ever.

At one time I did believe in women's ordination, but I've been more and more persuaded by the pope's reasoning.

Father Thomas Thompson, *of the International Marian Research Institute*

Over the course of centuries and into our own time, Mary has been used as a symbol to keep women in a certain cultural box, beneath the theological glass ceiling, to circumscribe the potential of women. Even Mary's virginity has been used for centuries as a model for women, telling them that marriage isn't everything, that virginal fidelity is a great model.

The ways of looking at Mary that makes her just a self-effacing obedient woman, whose whole dignity and glory and self-fulfillment reside in the fact that she was Mother of Jesus—that has to change. It has to change because the culture is demanding that it change.

Father Richard McBrien, *of Notre Dame*

The dictatorship of the pope in the Catholic Church makes the Catholic Church a male church without any possibility for women. The same dictatorship with a slightly different accent is the dictatorship of the Scripture: the Bible as the word of God. The Jewish roots of Christianity means that both Christianity and Judaism are sexist. No woman is allowed to have a position above a man. So they are all sexist, the whole Bible is more or less sexist—Old Testament, New Testament. Sometimes you hear a Catholic bishop cropping up and saying, "Christianity has liberated women." It's an invention to think that Christianity did anything for women.

Uta Ranke Heinemann, *author of* Eunuchs for the Kingdom of Heaven *and* Putting Away Childish Things

The pope is out of touch with understanding the concerns of Western women today. There is an enormous gender gap, because the pope is the product of an overwhelming male system. Mother Church and the Virgin Mary also are dominated by a male-oriented church. Now, there ain't no such thing as separate but equal because if you are separate you are not equal, and women do not have access to power

West Spring Street, Tisbury, Rez Williams

in the Roman Catholic Church because power is in ordination. The only way you get to be the pope is to get to be a priest. I think the Roman Catholic Church flirts with feminine principles it can tolerate, but can't deal with real women who demand equal rights and power.

Bishop John Spong, *author of* Born of a Woman

I am asked after lectures: How can you be a "liberal" on such matters as the rights of women, and still support an image that has been used to keep women in their place by a chauvinist, patriarchal church for two millennia? I reply that it is precisely because of the image of Mary that I support full equality for women and especially their ordination.

Father Andrew Greeley, *sociologist and author*

Mary and Elizabeth, Tanja Butler

If archaeologists were to come back two thousand years from now and find all these images of Mary in churches, they'd say, "Wow, that must have been a very feminist, woman-oriented society!"

Maurice Hamington, *feminist theologian, author of* Hail Mary?

I personally believe that the healthiest approach to Mary—the biblical Mary—is to appreciate her as a faithful woman of her time and place, a woman of prayer and reflection, living her life in service to her God and her community the best way she knew how. This is a more honest and appealing model, and one worth emulating for both women and men in today's world.

Andrea M. Johnson, *national coordinator, Women's Ordination Conference*

There's another side to Mary, the Mary of the Magnificat, the prayer she uttered when her cousin Elizabeth came to visit her. She says my soul magnifies the Lord, and my spirit rejoices in God my Savior. That's a prayer that talks about God bringing down the mighty from their thrones and lifting up the poor, a God of justice reaching out to the powerless. That's a side of Mary that, unfortunately, Catholic piety and devotion hasn't emphasized very much. The only place that aspect of Mary has been emphasized in recent time is in Latin America—in the so-called Latin American liberation theology.

The Mary of the Magnificat is a much more modern model, a strong woman who is not just interested in the house, but in justice and the poor, who realizes that we have to collaborate with a just God in working for justice in the world.

Father Richard McBrien, *of Notre Dame, author of* Catholicism

And Mary said, My soul doth magnify the Lord,

And my spirit hath rejoiced in God my Saviour.

For he hath regarded the low estate of his handmaiden: for, behold, from henceforth all generations shall call me blessed.

For he that is mighty hath done to me great things; and holy is his name,

And his mercy is on them that fear him from generation to generation.

He hath shewed strength with his arm; he hath scattered the proud in the imagination of their hearts.

He hath put down the mighty from their seats, and exalted them of low degree.

He hath filled the hungry with good things; and the rich he hath sent empty away.

He hath holpen his servant Israel, in remembrance of his mercy;

As he spake to our fathers, to Abraham, and to his seed for ever.

Luke 1:46-55, *Mary's "Magnificat" or the "Canticle of Mary"*

Madonna della Misericordia, Anonymous

Like all Italian girls, I was given a statue of the Virgin to keep on my bedside table. It was the generic blue-robed beatific-faced young lady, with a tin crown that I loved and played with as if it was some celestial Barbie.

The first time I brought a real live boy up to my room—I was probably about fourteen and snuck him in when my parents were away on a Saturday afternoon—I couldn't help but think that Mary was watching and disapproving. I really had the sense that she was there, and I was so uncomfortable that I couldn't fully concentrate on what was, at that point, new enough to need my full attention.

Finally, I excused myself, disengaged myself from the kissing—not to return to innocence but in order to put the statue outside my door where Mary couldn't see. Somehow, I felt that if she wasn't actually watching, it wouldn't count.

This mentality explains, I think, why I have been in therapy for a very long time.

Regina Barreca, *of the University of Connecticut*

In politics, *La Virgencita*, as she is known in Mexico, stands for the ability of the weak to triumph over the strong. She stands as proof that people without political power can gain victory over people with power. In history, Mexico's war for independence from Spain began in 1810 with these words from The Shout of Sorrows: "Long live the Virgin of Guadalupe and death to bad government." Every year during Mexican Independence Day celebrations, Mexicans still repeat this cry and honor the power of Our Lady of Guadalupe to unify people of diverse political backgrounds.

In folk history, *La Virgencita* is a powerful, positive symbol of the origin of the Mexican people. Like Mexicans themselves, Our Lady of Guadalupe began as a complex blend of Indian and European traditions.

Socially, Our Lady represents equality and acceptance for all people everywhere, no matter what their ethnic or socio-economic background. She symbolizes the common bond that unites all human beings.

In humanistic psychology, Our Lady stands for the power of persistence, forgiveness and love. She also represents the integration of the female and male components of the human psyche.

In feminist terms, Our Lady of Guadalupe embodies the power of women. Around the United States and beyond, when Hispanics celebrate the Day of Our Lady of Guadalupe on December 12, you

Virgin of Guadalupe, Rufino Tamayo

will hear among the vivas, "*Viva la mujer hispana!*"—long live the Hispanic woman! Many non-Hispanic women in the United States and beyond who have no formal connection to Catholicism admire and respect Our Lady of Guadalupe. For them, she is a source of comfort and strength.

Tonantzin Guadalupe, Lena Bartula

For people everywhere, regardless of their religious backgrounds, Our Lady is a healing antidote to the one-sided male theology of both Jewish and Protestant traditions. *¡Que viva La Virgencita!*

Susan Hazen-Hammond, *author of* Timelines of Native American History

In my part of the country, we're talking about the Virgin of Guadalupe. She wasn't protectoress of the Indians in her first century, it was the *criollos*, or Mexican-born Spaniards. But she drifted down the social scale as poorer people needed protecting. She transcends Catholicism now. She's become an ethnic identity symbol. Every time Chavez's farmworkers marched, she was right there. One scholar says that we Mexicans are not Christians, we're Marians, and that is totally true.

Now, word on the street is that one of the major drug lords in northern Sonora commissioned a thirty-foot-tall Our Lady of Guadalupe on a cement roadcut. She's etched into the windows and painted on the sides of low-riders. It gets interesting.

Jim Griffith, *Director of the Southwest Folklore Center
at the University of Arizona, Tucson*

Consider the place she occupies in the Koran. She is not only the most important woman in the Koran—more important than Hegar—but she receives a kind of attention as a human being that even the Prophet doesn't have. It's arguable that she's the most important person in the entire Koran. So much so, that when the early Christian opponents of Islam in the seventh and eighth centuries wanted to attack Islam and got translations of the Koran into Greek, they were astonished and somewhat nonplussed because here were these infidels who spoke in such glowing terms about Mary—not calling her Mother of God, but giving her a great centrality.

It is difficult, if not impossible, to imagine an individual life or a specific culture for which she is not an appropriate—and treasured—symbol. Her devotees are a remarkably kaleidoscopic group, from Dante and Mozart to Juan Diego of Guadalupe, from empresses and queens to illiterate girls to whom she appeared at Fatima and Lourdes. She fits everywhere, and offers something to everyone. Like no other figure, Mary appeals to both the emotional and the intellectual level, for she is no more than human, but blessed among women.

Jaroslav Pelikan, *of Yale, author of* Mary Through the Centuries

What is so important about Our Lady is that she suffered. This is an indispensable part for anyone who suffers through oppression, indispensable for any black person of any religious denomination in the United States—and in particular for black Catholics in this area. She's the person you can identify with completely. She was a woman, on the lowest rung of the ladder in the Jewish society. A woman who was not married, and who found herself—very mysteriously, very miraculously—to be with child, a child who would be the Son of God. She didn't understand it. Her "yes" was something that was an expression of trust in God, trust in the mysterious, that in some very mysterious way this was all going to work out. You can see it in black Catholic women in this area who have suffered tremendously throughout their lives, yet who seem to be so much at peace. They have suffered through so much hard work, they have seen children die, seen children slapped down by the racism that was a part of the deep South up until only recently. You see these women who are tremendous examples to the young people, they are devoted to prayer, to being very peaceful, and doing very peaceful, simple, ordinary things, knowing they have sent their children on their way for better or for worse. And they hold up the Blessed Mother as their example—as one who suffered through very difficult times, having had to face her son crucified on the cross. Mary may have believed that this end was wrong and misplaced, but she never wavered in her faith, and she was able to live and see the resurrection and see the glory, and she died a very peaceful woman. That is the dream of all Catholic women who suffer, and in particular the women in this area.

Greg Simien, *divinity student from Louisiana*

She's just so important to so many women. I can't emphasize enough that her imagery is more important in many parts of the world than Jesus' is.

Maurice Hamington, *feminist theologian, author of* Hail Mary?

Mother Mary

Karen Armstrong, who is in the very top rank of religious historians, was for seven years a Roman Catholic nun. But she had problems with the Virgin Mother: "In my convent there was a lot of that sickly stuff, a lot of horrible simpering Madonnas around, the white, gentile-looking lady. Never Semitic, which of course she really was. The whole Mary cult, when I was a girl, left me cold. We had to say the rosary every day after tea, and I hated it. A lot of the young nuns were quite taken with Mary, but I was more of a God girl."

And yet there was one version of the Virgin that she always found compelling. "The primordial picture of the mother with her child has been a good counterbalance in a male religion," she says. "The image of the mother—it's a strong one, an ancient one, a powerful one. The Church has been concerned at times that people are considering her more important than Jesus. That's how hugely the Mother Mary looms in the imagination."

Of Catholics, anyway. What about for others?

One of the intriguing aspects of the latest rise of Mary is this: The emotional need for her is so irresistible to a troubled world that people without an obvious link to the Virgin are being drawn to her. It's not news that Muslims revere Mary as a pure and holy saint—as Jaroslav Pelikan alluded, she's mentioned thirty-four times in the Koran, which upholds her virginal conception of Jesus—but to see large numbers of Muslims making pilgrimages to Christian Marian shrines is a remarkable thing. Interdenominational Marian prayer groups are springing up throughout the world. Many Protestants,

Celebration Song, Louise Brierley

even some who still reject notions of a supernatural Virgin, miss Mary. "I envy Catholicism its Mary," says Forrest Church, raised a Catholic but now a Unitarian minister. "Protestantism has nothing that can replace the part that she could or might play in their churches. She lends the idea of God a feminine face and makes the idea more available, less exclusionary."

LIFE *magazine, December 1996*

I think everybody needs to know that God loves us both like a father and a mother. And the Mary metaphor reflects this. The way that a mother loves a newborn child whom she's holding in her arms and is about to nurse—that's the way God loves us.

Father Andrew Greeley, *sociologist and author*

The Virgin of the Apocalypse Surrounded by Fire, Master, Book of Reason of Wolfegg

I can remember my grandmother, at a certain time at night, sitting in her chair before she retired for the day, with her book, giving due to God, in the way that the Blessed Mother showed devotion to God. All young men who are Catholic would identify and see the Blessed Mother in their mothers.

Greg Simien, *divinity student*

What is needed now for the preservation of the planet is the reintegration of the lost feminine. We have lost so much of the sacred feminine. We've lost the feminine love of nature, and of intuition and reverence and intimacy and tenderness and all of the things that belong to the sacred feminine. Christ's experience was not merely of the father but really also of the mother. And that experience came to Him through His own mother who was the incarnation of the divine motherhood of God and who sustained Him, educated Him, supported Him, witnessed His agony at the crucifixion, fed Him her strength, and went on to witness Him after the resurrection and to bind the whole church together by her presence and then was taken up into glory with Him. An astonishing journey, and amazing story.

Andrew Harvey, *author of* Mary's Vineyard

I think Mary is a particularly important figure for girls and women who don't have actual mothers present in their lives. My mother died when I was sixteen and I pretty much date my loss of conventional faith from that point. But I also remember sitting alone in the cramped and tacky suburban church after the funeral of my mother, crying at the statue of Mary, yelling at her as if she were the mother who, in dying, had abandoned me, as if Mary herself had let me down. Now, when I remember the moment—painful enough a moment that this doesn't happen very often, I admit—what strikes me most is that I still felt, back then, some sort of connection to Mother Mary. In my heart I railed at her the way I would have had my mother been present.

Thirty-five years later, I still bring—in my heart, not in a church—my best accomplishments and worst losses to the figure of Mary.

Regina Barreca, *of the University of Connecticut*

According to Pope Pius X, Mary did not stand lost in pain but joyfully at the cross of her son. John Paul II says that Mary at the cross lovingly consented in a maternal spirit to the sacrifice of the victim she had borne.

Well, I want to say there is no mother existing all over the world who stands joyfully beneath the gallows of her own son. That does not exist. And women who think about Mary do not imagine these things.

It's horrible what theology—bachelor theology—has done with Mary.

Mary, for me, is one who suffered by execution and killing. If we would follow her, we would be against every war, every killing, every death penalty.

Uta Ranke Heinemann, *author of* Eunuchs for the Kingdom of Heaven *and* Putting Away Childish Things

Now there stood by the cross of Jesus His mother, and His mother's sister, Mary the wife of Cleophas, and Mary Magdalene.

When Jesus therefore saw His mother, and the disciple standing by whom He loved, He saith unto His mother, Woman, behold thy son!

John 19:26-30

In Mallet—our town in Louisiana—the month of May is usually a month of reflection on the Blessed Mother and her part in the whole heavenly thing. People bring flowers and put them on the graves. If a mother has a child that died, she pays tribute on different days in the month of May. Mary was a great example of a mother. She would understand losing a child.

Terrance Simien, *zydeco recording artist*

Madonna and Child, Jesus Guerrero Galvan

Mary's role today should be as model for motherhood and for faith. Gabriel said she's above all women. I believe God meant that she be honored as an example for all mothers in her caring for her children, in her constant faith and in her service. Mary was a strong woman. She had to be, to have endured what life handed her. The mother of Jesus—what a responsibility! She had to keep Him safe, teach Him properly, give Him the support He needed as He faced His ministry on Earth. What a heartache!

What You Gonna Name That Pretty Little Baby?, Aminah Brenda Lynn Robinson

I identify with Mary. I raised seven children in times only slightly less troublesome than then. As a mother, I feel her heartache when her other sons did not believe in Jesus, when Jesus did not seem to be following God's will—that He be king, instead of serving as a medical missionary. I can imagine her humiliation, terror, anger as her son was arrested and unjustly killed.

Patricia Pfeiffer, *author of the novel*
Above All Women: The Story of the Virgin Mary

Madonna and Child, Jerzy Marek

When the prophet scoured out all of the graven images in the Ka'aba in Mecca, He left the image of the Virgin and child. And one of His last and most mysterious sayings was: Paradise is at the feet of the mothers. Mary could be the place where Islam and Christianity might meet. The hearts of the two faiths could be united.

Andrew Harvey, *author of* Mary's Vineyard

Mother of Divine Grace, unknown

I think Protestants are much more open to the idea of Mary now—the Biblical notion of Mary the Mother. At least you can talk about it now. They have some Marian hymns in their hymnals. It's extraordinary. The Methodist hymnal has a beautiful Marian hymn in it, and one of the Presbyterian hymnals has a nice advent hymn in it to Mary. Very small things, but…

As long as we don't present Mary as being another Jesus Christ, Protestantism is quite willing to take the biblical image of Mary. Their argument was always that we were making Mary another God.

Father Thomas Thompson, *of the International Marian Research Institute*

It's not a question of having no females in the Protestant church. On Easter morning, it was the females who were there with Christ. Rather it's the idea that Protestantism, by its rejection of the traditional Catholic views, deprived itself of the symbolism and ideas associated with Mary and is in that sense less able to articulate the feminine dimension of a God who is beyond gender.

Jaroslav Pelikan, *of Yale, author of* Mary Through the Centuries

There is a great deal of confusion about what to do about Mary. A lot of women just want to say let's just chuck that image, there's so much baggage that goes along with it. But on the other hand, this is the most powerful female figure in Western tradition. Getting rid of that is eliminating such an important female figure. Why not try to utilize it? So there isn't a great deal of agreement about what to do about Mary.

Maurice Hamington, *feminist theologian, author of* Hail Mary?

The beginning of the third millennium—by Christian count—has been portrayed by some as a crucial moment for world religions, during which they either will practice greater tolerance for one another and explore a liberating ecumenism or retreat into a fundamentalism bordering on tribalism. A central figure in the Christian aspect of this drama will be Mary. Her importance lies not merely in her recognition by other traditions—although it is well worth noting that she is the subject of one of the longer verses in the Koran. Rather, it is the openness

Madonna and Child, Claudia Porges Holland

of her embrace—what Jaroslav Pelikan has called her message of "both/and" rather than "either/or"—that may lead those who love her into a crucial understanding with non-Christians.

David Van Biema, *Senior Writer of Religion and other topics,* Time *magazine*

A Future Mary?

As we have seen, so many people—so many of them so different from one another—feel a need for Mary. This leads us to wonder, and to dream.

Forrest Church, the Unitarian minister and theologian from New York City, has a dream—of a middle-ground Mary, an Everymary who can transcend ideologies and give this tumultuous world the mother it needs. "I would like to think that she could be a bridge between religions," he says. "Not right now, perhaps. Those hymns to her in Protestant hymn books—I wonder how many times they get sung. But someday, if we could get back to a human Mary who is like us, who represents our mothers, I think we can come together through Mary. Think about it."

An entirely human Mary.

Ave Maria, gratia plena,

Dominus tecum, benedicta tu in mulieribus,

Et benedictus fructus ventris tui, Jesus…

I put on a Christmas CD and sit with a glass of unconsecrated wine, relaxing a bit and thinking about Forrest Church's Mary. Such a Mary, in a world we cannot see, might lead to an ecumenical reunion of Christian churches. Perhaps. It might even lead to a closer understanding of the teenage girl who gave birth in Bethlehem two thousand years ago. We could come to know Mary.

Sancta Maria, Mater Dei,

Ora pro nobis peccatoribus,

Nunc et in hora mortis nostrae.

Amen.

Think about it, Forrest Church urged. And so I do. I think about what I've learned since I learned that first "Hail Mary." I think of Mary singing psalms in the synagogue. Can we ask this simple girl to guide what has become not a cult but a huge and passionate congregation, a movement requiring a heroine, a worldwide flock that has long demanded more of her? That has demanded, in some instances, that she deliver her message herself? That has demanded this even unto signs, even unto appearances?

I wonder: If Mary became merely human—if people could truly touch Mary—would Mary be enough?

Robert Sullivan, LIFE magazine, December 1996

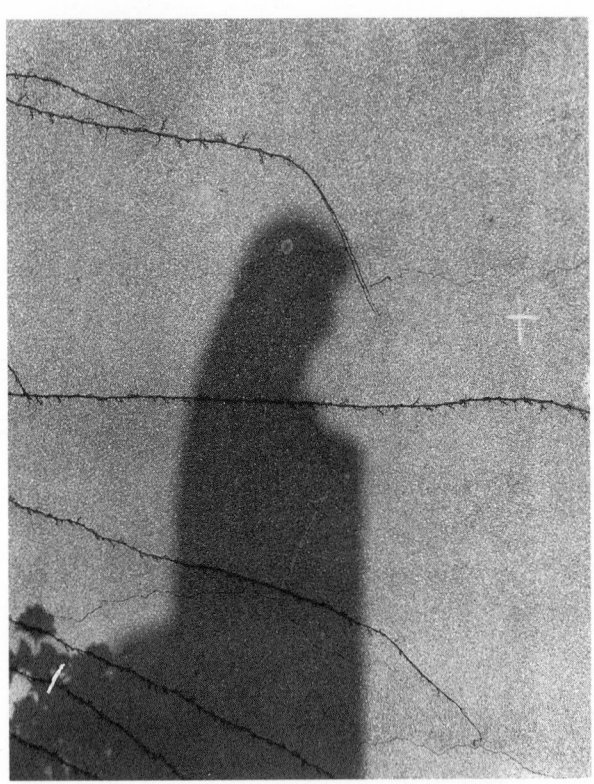

Untitled, Eryk Hanut